PRACTICAL GUIDE:
ENGINEERING IN BRIEF

BY AYOUB SADDIK

The IN BRIEF collection is a small manual for non-experts.

TABLE OF CONTENTS

Introduction..5
List of Main Branches...................................7
Brief Description of Main Branches..............8
Civil Engineering..13
Mechanical Engineering............................15
Electrical Engineering...............................17
Computer Engineering..............................19
Aerospace Engineering.............................21
Chemical Engineering...............................24
Environmental Engineering.......................27
Materials Engineering...............................30
Biomedical Engineering............................33
Nuclear Engineering.................................36
Industrial Engineering...............................38
Marine Engineering..................................40
Software Engineering...............................42
Petroleum and Gas Engineering..............45
Agricultural Engineering...........................47
Geotechnical Engineering........................49
Telecommunications Engineering............52
Production Engineering...........................55
Conclusion...57

INTRODUCTION

Engineering is a discipline that deals with the application of scientific and mathematical principles to design, build, and maintain structures, machinery, systems, and technological processes. Engineers use their knowledge of these disciplines to solve complex technical problems and create innovative solutions to improve people's lives and the environment.

Engineering is a very broad field and includes various specializations, including civil, mechanical, electrical, computer, aerospace, environmental, and many others. Engineers can work in various sectors, such as designing and constructing bridges, buildings, cars, airplanes, electronics, computer science, energy, manufacturing, and many other areas.

Engineering requires a strong knowledge of mathematics, physics, and sciences, as well as problem-solving skills, critical thinking, and creativity. Engineers must also be able to communicate and work in teams, as they often collaborate with other professionals and specialists.

LIST OF MAIN BRANCHES:

1. Civil Engineering
2. Mechanical Engineering
3. Electrical Engineering
4. Computer Engineering
5. Aerospace Engineering
6. Chemical Engineering
7. Environmental Engineering
8. Materials Engineering
9. Biomedical Engineering
10. Nuclear Engineering
11. Industrial Engineering
12. Marine Engineering
13. Software Engineering
14. Petroleum and Gas Engineering
15. Agricultural Engineering
16. Geotechnical Engineering
17. Telecommunications Engineering
18. Production Engineering.

SHORT DESCRIPTION OF THE
MAIN BRANCHES

Here is a brief description of each engineering discipline:

Civil Engineering: deals with the design, construction, and maintenance of infrastructure such as bridges, roads, dams, buildings, hydraulic systems, sewer systems, and more.

Mechanical Engineering: deals with the design, development, and maintenance of mechanical systems such as engines, turbines, transmission systems, industrial machinery, construction equipment, and more.

Electrical Engineering: deals with the design, development, and maintenance of electrical systems and devices such as generators, transformers, power distribution networks, control equipment, medical devices, and more.

Computer Engineering: deals with the design, development, and maintenance of computer systems, software, hardware, and networks such as web applications, data processing programs, mobile devices, cybersecurity systems, and more.

Aerospace Engineering: deals with the design, development, and maintenance of aerospace systems and technologies such as airplanes, helicopters, satellites, spacecraft, and more.

Chemical Engineering: deals with the design, development, and maintenance of chemical processes such as the production of drugs, food, fuel, synthetic materials, chemicals, and more.

Environmental Engineering: deals with the design, development, and maintenance of systems and technologies for environmental protection such as waste management, soil remediation, water treatment, and more.

Materials Engineering: deals with the design, development, and production of advanced materials for specific applications such as metal alloys, composite materials, ceramics, polymers, and more.

Biomedical Engineering: deals with the design, development, and maintenance of medical devices, hospital equipment, and health technologies such as pacemakers, prosthetics, diagnostic tools, imaging equipment, and more.

Nuclear Engineering: deals with the design, development, and maintenance of technologies and facilities that use nuclear energy such as nuclear power plants, reactors, medical devices, and more.

Industrial Engineering: deals with the design, development, and management of production systems and industrial processes such as assembly lines, quality management systems, resource optimization, and more.

Marine Engineering: deals with the design, construction, and maintenance of ships, boats, ports, offshore installations, maritime safety systems, and more.

Software Engineering: deals with the design, development, and maintenance of software, applications, and computer systems such as data processing programs, web applications, enterprise management software, games, and more.

Petroleum and Gas Engineering: deals with the design, development, and maintenance of systems and technologies for the extraction, production, and distribution of oil and gas such as offshore platforms, refining plants, distribution networks, and more.

Agricultural Engineering: deals with the design, development, and management of systems and technologies for agriculture such as irrigation systems, agricultural machinery, cultivation techniques, agricultural biotechnology, and more.

Geotechnical Engineering: deals with the design, development, and management of systems and technologies for the study and management of land such as geology, geotechnics, geophysics, geochemistry, and more.

Telecommunications Engineering: deals with the design, development, and management of systems and technologies for communication such as telecommunications networks, data transmission systems, wireless communication devices, and more.

Production Engineering: deals with the design, development, and management of systems and technologies for the production of goods and services such as production planning, quality management, logistics, and more.

CHAPTER 1: CIVIL ENGINEERING

Civil Engineering deals with the design, construction, maintenance, and management of civil infrastructure and structures such as buildings, bridges, roads, dams, aqueducts, sewers, hydraulic systems, and much more.

Civil engineers work mainly in the construction sector but also in other sectors such as transportation, energy, and environment. Among the subjects studied in Civil Engineering are solid and structural mechanics, geotechnics, hydraulics, geology, urban planning, construction technology, resource management, and much more.

Civil engineers must possess advanced technical skills, project management skills, the ability to solve complex problems, as well as an in-depth knowledge of local and international regulations, laws, and regulations that concern the construction and civil engineering sector in general.

CHAPTER 2: MECHANICAL ENGINEERING

Mechanical engineering is a branch of engineering that deals with the design, development, production, and maintenance of mechanical systems and components. Mechanical engineers work in many sectors, including automotive, aerospace, industrial machinery manufacturing, medical device production, energy, environment, and many others.

Mechanical engineers engage in a wide range of activities, including designing mechanical components and systems, analyzing and simulating systems and components, selecting materials and production techniques, managing projects, maintaining and optimizing existing systems and components, implementing advanced technologies such as robotics and 3D printing, and much more.

The subjects of study in mechanical engineering include solid mechanics, thermodynamics, fluid mechanics, materials science, system dynamics, robotics, computer-aided design (CAD), computer-aided manufacturing (CAM), quality management, and much more.

Mechanical engineers must have a strong understanding of science and mathematics, as well as strong creativity and problem-solving skills. They must also possess advanced technical skills, project management abilities, a good understanding of local and international regulations and laws, and the ability to work well in teams.

CHAPTER 3: ELECTRICAL ENGINEERING

Electrical engineering is a branch of engineering that deals with the study, design, production, and management of electrical and electronic systems and devices. Electrical engineers work in many sectors, including energy, telecommunications, industrial automation, consumer electronics, transportation, and many others.

Electrical engineers engage in a wide range of activities, including designing electrical and electronic circuits, designing power systems, designing control systems, analyzing and simulating electrical and electronic systems, managing projects, maintaining and optimizing existing electrical and electronic systems, researching and developing new technologies, and much more.

The subjects of study in electrical engineering include electrical engineering, electronics, signal theory, circuit theory, systems theory, programming, robotics, control theory, safety of electrical and electronic systems, and much more.

Electrical engineers must have a strong understanding of science and mathematics, as well as strong creativity and problem-solving skills. They must also possess advanced technical skills, project management abilities, a good understanding of local and international regulations and laws, and the ability to work well in teams.

CHAPTER 4: COMPUTER ENGINEERING

Computer Engineering is a branch of engineering that deals with the study, design, production, and management of computer systems and software. Computer engineers work in many sectors, including industry, commerce, finance, health, transportation, education, and many others.

Computer engineers engage in a wide range of activities, including designing computer systems, designing software, programming, developing web and mobile applications, managing software projects, computer security, data analysis, research and development of new technologies, and much more.

Subjects studied in Computer Engineering include programming, algorithms and data structures, databases, computer networks, computer security, artificial intelligence, systems theory, robotics, and much more.

Computer engineers must have a solid knowledge of mathematics and computer science, as well as strong creativity and problem-solving skills. They must also possess advanced technical skills, project management skills, a good understanding of local and international laws and regulations, and good teamwork skills.

CHAPTER 5: AEROSPACE ENGINEERING

Aerospace Engineering is a branch of engineering that deals with the design, development, construction, and management of aircraft, spacecraft, satellites, and ground support systems. In other words, aerospace engineers are involved in all phases of the life cycle of an aircraft or spacecraft, from initial design to construction, testing, operations, and maintenance.

Aerospace engineers must have a deep understanding of physics, mathematics, materials science, electronics, and computer science, as these elements are essential in designing and building safe and efficient aircraft and spacecraft.

The main areas of specialization in aerospace engineering include:

Aerodynamics: studies the behavior of fluids around objects in motion, particularly aircraft.

Propulsion: focuses on the design and development of engines for aircraft and spacecraft.

Structures: studies the materials and construction techniques used to build aircraft and spacecraft.

Control and navigation: deals with the guidance, navigation, and control systems used to manage aircraft and spacecraft.

Space systems: focuses on the design and development of satellites, probes, and spacecraft for exploration and observation missions.

In summary, Aerospace Engineering is a discipline that requires a solid understanding of physics, mathematics, materials science, and computer science, along with a strong passion for aviation and space exploration. Aerospace engineers often work in multidisciplinary teams to design and build complex and innovative vehicles and systems, contributing to our understanding of the universe and our world.

CHAPTER 6: CHEMICAL ENGINEERING

Chemical Engineering is a branch of engineering that deals with designing, developing, and managing industrial processes that involve the transformation of raw materials into finished products using principles of chemistry, physics, mathematics, and engineering.

Chemical engineers work on industrial processes that involve the production of chemicals, pharmaceuticals, food, beverages, fuels, electronic materials, personal care products, and other consumer goods. These processes may include chemical synthesis, purification of chemicals, component separation, mixing, chemical reactivity, and process control.

Some of the main areas of specialization in Chemical Engineering include:

Chemical process engineering: which deals with designing, developing, and managing industrial chemical processes.

Chemical reaction engineering: which studies chemical reactions and their industrial applications.

Materials engineering: which focuses on designing, developing, and producing new materials and new applications for existing materials.

Environmental engineering: which deals with managing natural resources, protecting the environment, and developing eco-friendly technologies.

Chemical engineers often work in multidisciplinary teams with other professionals such as scientists, technicians, and production operators to design and develop efficient and sustainable industrial processes. Their skills are required in many sectors such as the chemical industry, pharmaceuticals, food, energy production, materials industry, and other sectors where industrial production is important.

In summary, Chemical Engineering is a discipline that requires a strong understanding of chemistry, physics, mathematics, and engineering, along with a passion for researching and designing sustainable and innovative industrial processes. Chemical engineers play a crucial role in creating products and technologies that improve people's lives and contribute to economic growth and sustainable development of society.

CHAPTER 7: ENVIRONMENTAL ENGINEERING

Environmental Engineering is a branch of engineering that focuses on developing sustainable and innovative solutions to environmental problems. Environmental engineers work on issues related to air, water, and soil quality, waste management, energy sustainability, climate change, and biodiversity protection.

Among the key areas of specialization in Environmental Engineering are:

Waste Management: which focuses on the management of solid, liquid, and gaseous waste, including their disposal, recycling, and reduction.

Air and Water Quality: which deals with monitoring and improving air and water quality through the management of pollution sources and the promotion of low-impact environmental technologies.

Energy Sustainability: which focuses on the design and development of low-impact environmental energy technologies, such as solar, wind, and geothermal energy.

Environmental Impact: which studies the effects of human activities on the environment, such as infrastructure construction, urban development, and agriculture.

Biodiversity and Conservation: which focuses on the conservation of biodiversity through the management of natural ecosystems, the protection of wildlife and plant species, and the promotion of sustainable agricultural practices.

Environmental engineers often work in multidisciplinary teams with other professionals such as biologists, chemists, geologists, and urban planners to design and develop sustainable solutions to environmental problems. Their skills are in demand in many sectors including industry, agriculture, natural resource management, urban planning, and environmental policy.

In summary, Environmental Engineering is a discipline that requires a solid understanding of environmental science, physics, mathematics, and engineering, along with a passion for environmental sustainability and protection. Environmental engineers play a crucial role in finding innovative solutions to environmental problems, contributing to the creation of a more sustainable world in harmony with nature.

CHAPTER 8: MATERIALS ENGINEERING

Materials Engineering is a branch of engineering that deals with the study and design of advanced materials for industry. The main objective of Materials Engineering is to develop innovative materials with specific properties that can meet the needs of a wide range of applications, from the aerospace industry to the biomedical field.

Materials engineers use knowledge of the atomic and molecular properties of materials to design and develop new materials or improve existing ones. Some of the main areas of specialization in Materials Engineering include:

Metallic materials: which focus on the development of new metal alloys with specific properties, such as corrosion resistance or the ability to withstand high temperatures.

Ceramic materials: which deal with the design of advanced ceramic materials for high-temperature applications, such as the production of refractories or the creation of energy production facilities.

Polymeric materials: which concentrate on the development of new polymeric materials, such as high-performance plastics, used in various industrial applications, such as the automotive, electronics, textile, and 3D printing industries.

Composite materials: which deal with the development of composite materials, such as carbon fibers or Kevlar, used to improve the strength and lightweight of products such as vehicles, aircraft, and sports equipment.

Energy materials: which focus on the design of new materials for energy production and storage, such as lithium-ion batteries or fuel cells.

Materials engineers work in a wide range of industrial sectors, including the aerospace, automotive, electronics, energy, biomedical, and general manufacturing industries. Their work often involves collaboration with other engineers and scientists, such as physicists, chemists, and biologists, to develop innovative solutions for the technological challenges of the future.

In summary, Materials Engineering is a highly interdisciplinary discipline that requires in-depth knowledge of chemistry, physics, materials science, and engineering. Materials engineers play a crucial role in the development of new advanced materials, contributing to technological innovation in various sectors and the creation of increasingly safe, efficient, and sustainable products.

CHAPTER 9: BIOMEDICAL ENGINEERING

Biomedical Engineering is a branch of engineering that focuses on the design and development of medical devices and instrumentation for monitoring and diagnostics, as well as the creation of advanced therapies and technological solutions to improve people's health and quality of life.

Biomedical Engineering combines principles of biology, medicine, computer science, electronics, and mechanics to develop technical solutions for complex medical problems. Biomedical engineers work on a wide range of applications, from designing medical devices such as pacemakers, electronic prosthetics, and implants, to medical imaging systems such as computed tomography and magnetic resonance imaging, and developing software for the analysis and interpretation of biomedical data.

Biomedical Engineering is one of the most important and rapidly growing fields of modern engineering, with applications in many areas of medicine, including early disease diagnosis, advanced therapy, personalized medicine, and digital health.

Biomedical engineers must be able to apply their scientific and engineering knowledge to solve specific medical problems, but they must also understand the needs of patients and medical professionals. In addition, they must be able to work collaboratively with doctors, researchers, and other health professionals to develop innovative and advanced solutions.

Some areas of specialization in Biomedical Engineering include:

Bioengineering: which focuses on the design of medical devices such as prosthetics, implants, pacemakers, electrostimulators, and diagnostic equipment, such as imaging tools.

Tissue and Regenerative Engineering: which focuses on designing new tissues and organs for regeneration and transplantation.

Medical Informatics: which deals with creating software for the analysis of biomedical data, simulation of biological processes, and processing of medical images.

Biomechanical Engineering: which focuses on understanding the biomechanical processes of the human body and designing prosthetics and implants that can reproduce these functions.

Medical Devices for Digital Health: which deals with designing advanced monitoring and diagnostic solutions, such as apps and wearable devices.

In conclusion, Biomedical Engineering is a discipline that requires a strong background in natural sciences, technology, and medicine. Biomedical engineers are at the forefront of the fight against diseases and the promotion of health, using their scientific and technological knowledge to develop innovative and advanced solutions that improve people's lives.

CHAPTER 10: NUCLEAR ENGINEERING

Nuclear engineering is a branch of engineering that deals with the design, development, implementation, and use of technologies and systems that involve the atomic nucleus to produce energy or perform other activities.

One of the main fields of application of nuclear engineering is the production of electricity through nuclear fission. This process harnesses the energy released by the separation of atomic nuclei within a nuclear reactor, which is then used to generate steam and move turbines, thereby producing electricity.

Nuclear engineering is also used in other applications such as the production of radioisotopes for medical use, the management of radioactive waste, nuclear safety, and national defense.

Nuclear engineers must have a thorough understanding of nuclear physics, thermodynamics, fluid mechanics, and electronics, as well as a detailed knowledge of the materials and engineering techniques necessary to design and build nuclear systems.

Moreover, safety is a central concern in nuclear engineering, so nuclear engineers must be highly skilled in risk management, safety system design, and safety assessment of existing systems.

In summary, nuclear engineering is a discipline that deals with the application of nuclear physics for the production of electricity and other uses, and requires a deep understanding of numerous scientific and engineering disciplines, as well as an impeccable focus on safety and risk management.

CHAPTER 11: INDUSTRIAL ENGINEERING

Industrial Engineering is a branch of Engineering that focuses on the design, development, implementation, and optimization of industrial production systems. This discipline combines technical knowledge and data analysis to improve the efficiency and productivity of industrial processes.

Industrial engineers use process and plant analysis techniques to identify problems and improve productivity. This includes the study of time and methods, workflow analysis, layout optimization, and evaluation of technologies and materials used in production processes.

Furthermore, Industrial Engineering deals with organizational and management problems, such as resource planning, supply chain management, quality control, operations management, and production planning.

Industrial engineers work in various industries, including manufacturing, logistics, services, and healthcare. Their expertise is required to improve productivity, reduce costs, and increase the quality of products and services.

Moreover, Industrial Engineering focuses on the implementation of advanced technologies such as automation, robotics, the Internet of Things (IoT), and Artificial Intelligence (AI) to improve production processes and make the industry more efficient and sustainable.

In summary, Industrial Engineering is a discipline that uses technical knowledge and data analysis to improve the efficiency and productivity of production processes. Industrial engineers deal with organizational and management problems, as well as technical ones, and work in various industries to improve productivity and make the industry more efficient and sustainable.

CHAPTER 12: MARITIME ENGINEERING

Maritime Engineering is a branch of Engineering that deals with the design, construction, maintenance, and management of ships and maritime facilities. This discipline combines the technical knowledge of Engineering with the specific skills required for navigation in open sea.

Maritime engineers work on various aspects of ships and maritime facilities, including the design of ship structures, installation of propulsion systems, design of navigation systems, management of loading and unloading operations, maintenance of onboard equipment, and management of energy efficiency.

In addition, Maritime Engineering deals with the design and management of port infrastructure, such as docks, piers, ports, and container terminals, and other maritime infrastructure, such as safety and rescue systems.

Maritime engineers must have a deep understanding of marine material properties, dynamics of waves and marine currents, fluid mechanics, and shipbuilding technologies. They must also be able to manage risks associated with navigation in open sea and work in compliance with international maritime norms and regulations.

In summary, Maritime Engineering is a discipline that deals with the design, construction, maintenance, and management of ships and maritime facilities, and the management of port infrastructure and other maritime infrastructure. Maritime engineers must have a deep understanding of marine material properties, dynamics of waves and marine currents, and shipbuilding technologies, as well as be able to manage risks associated with navigation in open sea and work in compliance with international maritime norms and regulations.

CHAPTER 13: SOFTWARE ENGINEERING

Software Engineering is a discipline of Engineering that deals with the design, development, maintenance, and management of software. The main goal of Software Engineering is to produce high-quality, reliable, efficient, and secure software, using software development and lifecycle management methodologies.

Software engineers work on various aspects of software, including architecture design, code writing, testing and verification, project management, software maintenance, and customer support. Software Engineering is based on software development methodologies, such as the waterfall methodology, agile methodology, and DevOps methodology.

The waterfall methodology is a sequential model of software development, where each phase of the development process is completed before moving on to the next one. The agile methodology, on the other hand, is based on an iterative and incremental approach to software development, where the software is developed in small pieces, called sprints, and each sprint is continuously evaluated and improved.

Finally, the DevOps methodology focuses on collaboration and integration between software development and IT operations, with the goal of improving software efficiency, quality, and security.

Software engineers must have a deep understanding of programming languages, frameworks, and technologies used in software development. They must also have a good understanding of business processes and customer requirements in order to develop software that meets their needs.

In summary, Software Engineering is a discipline that deals with the design, development, maintenance, and management of software, using software development and lifecycle management methodologies. Software engineers must have a deep understanding of programming languages, frameworks, and technologies used in software development, as well as a good understanding of business processes and customer requirements.

CHAPTER 14: PETROLEUM AND GAS ENGINEERING

Petroleum and gas engineering is a branch of engineering that focuses on the production and exploitation of fossil fuels, such as oil and natural gas. This discipline deals with the extraction, transportation, refining, and distribution of oil and gas, as well as the design, construction, and management of production, storage, and transportation facilities.

Petroleum and gas engineers must have a deep understanding of the properties of fossil fuels, drilling and extraction techniques, refining and distribution processes, as well as safety and environmental impact associated with these activities. They must also be familiar with the technologies used for production measurement and control, such as telemetry systems and pressure sensors.

Petroleum and gas engineers work in various sectors, including the petroleum and gas industry, electric power, and engineering and consulting companies. They may be involved in designing and installing new production facilities, evaluating and optimizing existing activities, or managing risks and safety in the workplace. Additionally, petroleum and gas engineers may work in the field, where they deal with drilling, extraction, and plant maintenance operations.

In summary, petroleum and gas engineering is a discipline that requires advanced technological skills, scientific knowledge, and great attention to safety and environmental impact. Petroleum and gas engineers are engaged in the development of innovative technologies for the production and exploitation of fossil fuels, in order to ensure safe and efficient energy supply for the future.

CHAPTER 15: AGRICULTURAL ENGINEERING

Agricultural engineering is a discipline that focuses on the application of science and technology to agriculture. Agricultural engineers use their knowledge of agriculture, biological sciences, and information technologies to design, construct, and manage efficient and sustainable agricultural systems.

The main areas of interest in agricultural engineering include the design of agricultural machinery and equipment, water resource management, irrigation system design, soil and water conservation, greenhouse and controlled environment agriculture system design, biofuel production plant design, and agricultural waste management.

Agricultural engineers work closely with farmers, agronomists, and other agricultural experts to create technical solutions to the challenges that modern agriculture faces, such as increasing demand for food products, reducing the environmental impact of agriculture, sustainable management of natural resources, and adoption of innovative technologies.

Agricultural engineers can work in various sectors, including agriculture, food production, biofuel industry, government agencies, and environmental consulting firms. They may be involved in the design and installation of agricultural equipment, management of rural development projects, evaluation of the environmental impact of agricultural systems, or research and development of new technologies for sustainable agriculture.

In summary, agricultural engineering is a discipline that combines science and technology to develop innovative and sustainable solutions for modern agriculture. Agricultural engineers are committed to creating efficient, safe, and sustainable agricultural systems, ensuring safe and sustainable food supply for the future.

CHAPTER 16: GEOTECHNICAL ENGINEERING

Geotechnical engineering is a discipline that focuses on the application of engineering principles to the properties and behaviors of geological materials. Geotechnical engineers use their knowledge of geology, soil mechanics, and geotechnics to design, construct, and manage infrastructure that relies on the ground, such as bridges, roads, dams, buildings, tunnels, and other civil engineering works.

The main fields of interest in geotechnical engineering include the characterization of soils, the analysis of loads and deformations of the ground, the design of foundations, the design of retaining walls, the evaluation of seismic risk and slope stability, the design of containment structures, and the management of water resources.

Geotechnical engineers work closely with geologists, hydrologists, and other experts in the field to create technical solutions to the challenges that civil engineering must face, such as building infrastructure on difficult or unstable terrain, mitigating seismic risk, and protecting against natural events.

Geotechnical engineers can work in various sectors, including civil engineering, mining industry, oil and gas industry, government agencies, and environmental consulting firms. They may be involved in the design and installation of containment structures, the evaluation of soil stability, the management of water resources, or the research and development of new technologies for geotechnical engineering.

In summary, geotechnical engineering is a discipline that combines geology and engineering to develop innovative and safe solutions for building infrastructure on difficult or unstable terrain. Geotechnical engineers are committed to ensuring that civil infrastructure is safe, durable, and environmentally sustainable, in order to ensure a sustainable future for society.

CHAPTER 17: TELECOMMUNICATIONS ENGINEERING

Telecommunications engineering is a discipline that deals with the development, design, implementation, and management of communication and data transmission systems. In particular, telecommunications engineers design and manage communication networks, data transmission systems, satellite communication systems, wireless telecommunications systems, and optical communication systems.

The field of telecommunications engineering is broad and constantly evolving. Areas of interest include the design of telecommunications networks, the design and optimization of wireless communication systems, the design of satellite communication systems, the design of optical communication systems, the design of integrated circuits for communication, the design of encoding and decoding algorithms, network security, and the analysis of telecommunications system performance.

Telecommunications engineers often work closely with other professionals such as electronic, computer, physics, and mathematics engineers to create technical solutions to the challenges that modern communication must face. These challenges include the need to transmit large amounts of data efficiently, ensure the security of transmitted information, and meet the ever-increasing needs of users.

Telecommunications engineers can work in various sectors such as the design of communication systems for mobile telephony, the satellite industry, the design of communication systems for computer networks, and the design of telecommunications equipment.

In summary, telecommunications engineering is a discipline that focuses on the development and management of modern communication systems. Telecommunications engineers work to create innovative and secure solutions for data communication, which are essential for the global economy, scientific research, and people's daily lives.

CHAPTER 18: PRODUCTION ENGINEERING

Production Engineering is a discipline that deals with the study and organization of production processes, in order to improve their efficiency, productivity, and quality. Production engineers work to design, manage, and improve production processes, not only in traditional industrial sectors, but also in high-tech sectors such as information technology, electronics, and biotechnology.

The work of production engineers mainly consists of designing and developing new production processes, improving existing ones, and optimizing workflows, production times, human resources, and materials used.

Activities carried out by production engineers include defining production methods, planning and organizing production, defining production layouts, selecting machinery and tools used, managing costs, defining quality and safety parameters, and implementing production control systems.

Production engineers work in various industries, including automotive, aerospace, mechanical, chemical, and electronics. They can also work in service and consulting companies, the public sector, and academic institutions.

Production Engineering plays an important role in optimizing production processes, increasing efficiency and productivity, and reducing production costs. Thanks to their technical and managerial skills, production engineers contribute to the improvement of industry and the economy in general.

IN CONCLUSION

Engineering is a discipline that deals with the application of science, technology, and mathematical knowledge to solve real-world problems and create innovative solutions in various fields, from industry to the environment, from infrastructure to information and communication technologies.

Engineers, with their technical skills and problem-solving abilities, are able to design, build, manage, and improve the systems, processes, and technologies that form the basis of modern society. Engineering is a highly interdisciplinary discipline that requires knowledge of multiple areas of science, technology, and economics.

Engineering is divided into numerous specializations, including civil engineering, mechanical engineering, electrical engineering, chemical engineering, biomedical engineering, information engineering, environmental engineering, and many others. Each specialization focuses on a specific field of engineering application, but all share the same philosophy and methodology of work.

In summary, Engineering is a fundamental discipline for the development and prosperity of modern society, thanks to its ability to develop technical solutions to real-world problems and constantly innovate to improve the quality of life for people and the well-being of the environment we live in.

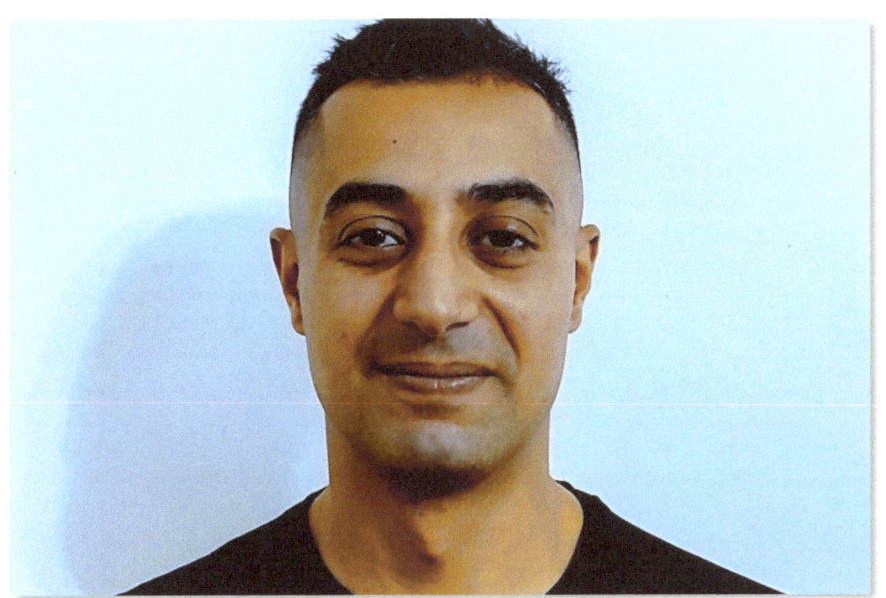

BIOGRAPHY

With my engineering curiosity, I wanted to share quick explanations about everyday topics, of which we don't always grasp the main points of the whole. I hope to have shed some light on the subject, goodbye! A big hug to all my loved ones who support and endure me! Thank you!

AD MAIORA SEMPER

Ingram Content Group UK Ltd.
Milton Keynes UK
UKHW051947140423
420143UK00004B/130